BOVEY TRACEY
IN BYGONE DAYS

A Portrait of a Dartmoor Town

Lance Tregoning

DEVON BOOKS

First published in Great Britain in 1989 by Devon Books

British Library Cataloguing-in-Publication Data
Tregoning, Lance
  Bovey Tracey in bygone days.
  1. Devon. Bovey Tracey, history
  I.Title
  942.3'55

ISBN: 0 86114–844–4

Printed and bound in Great Britain by A. Wheaton & Co. Ltd
Typeset in Great Britain by P&M Typesetting Ltd, Exeter

DEVON BOOKS
Official Publisher to Devon County Council
An imprint of Wheaton Publishers Ltd. A Member of Maxwell Pergamon
Publishing Corporation plc

Wheaton Publishers Ltd
Hennock Road, Marsh Barton, Exeter, Devon EX2 8RP
Tel: 0392 74121; Telex 42794 (WHEATN G)

SALES
Direct sales enquiries to Devon Books at the address above.

To my wife Minola for all her help

CONTENTS

About the Author

Lance Tregoning was born in 1917, in a house in East Street, known as Summerfields. It was run by his grandmother, Kate Farnes, as a Guest House. His parents had a grocer's shop in Town Hall Square. They later moved their business to the corner of Orchard Terrace, where they finally closed in 1963 when his father died.

Lance went to the old Church School until he was eleven years old, and then went to the Grammar School in Newton Abbot. After that, but not including the war years, he worked for nineteen years in the family business, learning every facet of the grocery trade. In those days, he says, it was far more skilful, diverse and interesting than the pre-packaged trade of today, but those days are sadly gone forever.

FOREWORD

This book is a pictorial record of Bovey Tracey as it was in the latter part of the last century and the early part of this.

I have always been interested in local history, and during my formative years I was fortunate enough to be able to see a great deal of the people and buildings in the town. My father had a grocer's shop in Bovey, and both my parents and grandmother, along with many older inhabitants, contributed to the mass of information I was able to acquire. By the 1950s it was becoming increasingly obvious that the face of the town was changing. I started taking photographs of the buildings and streets, whilst at the same time gathering together old photographs, of which I now have an ever growing collection of over 300. These I keep in albums, dated and named – preserved for posterity.

I begin the book by taking you on a walk through the old town. As you will see, a great many of the old landmarks are alas long gone. Following this, there are sections on schooling, leisure, work, festivities and so on, covering all the facets of a bygone age in a Devon town.

Perhaps this will prompt more memories from anyone able to recall those early years and hopefully show the younger generations just how the town used to be, how their ancestors lived and just what made Bovey Tracey such a good place to live in. As you read this book you will find that this sentiment is repeated again and again as is shown without exception in all the stories I heard from such a variety of people.

I am indebted to many people who, over the years, have either given or loaned me pictures and allowed me to have them copied. I wish to acknowledge the following people who loaned photographs especially for the book: Mrs Margaret Dadd, Mrs Isobel Bibbings, Mrs Marjorie Steer, Mr Peter Gray, Mrs Helen Mann, Mr Leonard Webber, Mr Bill Hodge, Mrs June Williams, Mrs Nancy Collins, Mrs Nora Davis, Mrs Hester Ralph, Bovey Cricket Club, Mr Arthur Weeks, Mrs Antry Distin and Miss Kate Tolley. Thanks are also due to Teignbridge Archive for their help, especially to Adrian Lyons, their photographer.

I hope this book will provide a permanent record of how the town used to be. Perhaps in future someone else will continue the story to a more recent era, and then we can compare the two.

LANCE TREGONING

A STROLL THROUGH THE OLD TOWN, BEGINNING AT DEVON HOUSE

At the turn of the century the town was very much smaller than it is now. In my lifetime I can remember when there were no houses to the east beyond the parish church, nothing but fields to the west of Mary Street and Hind Street, and just a handful of houses beyond St John's. The building boom began after the Second World War and the town has tripled in size over the last thirty years or so.

Devon House was built as a house of correction for wayward girls and orphans. Run by the Sisters of the House of Clewer, it was built in the period 1867–75 and was in use until the outbreak of the Second World War. The occupants were a familiar sight in Bovey, walking in crocodiles, in their distinctive dress, accompanied by the 'Sisters of Mercy'.

The Laundry.
Devon House of Mercy. Bovey Tracey.

Some of the girls at work in the laundry, the mainstay of the house. Note the washing troughs and mangle. The pictures date from around 1890. The picture above shows the ironing room.

The house contained a beautiful chapel which had its own chaplain.

The Church Cottages were built in 1490 for the secular use of the church such as meetings, meals, brewing of ale, etc. They were last owned by the church in 1580 and were sold for financial reasons.

The College in 1894. This was what the name implies, a college for training singers for the choir, servers and clerks. It was built in the fifteenth century by Lady Margaret Beaufort, mother of Henry VII, the Lady of the Manor at that time.

The group on the left of the picture are Mr Samuel Heath, his wife Liza and some of their children. In the doorway is Mrs Sam Heath and under the second window is Mr Charles Heath. In the centre of the group is Mr Charles Lethbridge who is holding H. Lethbridge and Miss Lethbridge by the hand. Alice Lethbridge is in the light dress. Mr Thomas Kelly is on the right in the tall hat.

The northern part of the college was demolished in 1896 to allow for the building of the Courtenay Memorial. The picture shows the plot after major demolition and before the building of the memorial ground.

The Courtenay Memorial is composed of an ancient Dartmoor stone cross. It was found by Canon Courtenay being used as one of the steps up to the church. Reinstated by him and set up in the churchyard, it was later moved to its present position as his memorial.

The top half of East Street around 1900, before Moorlands was built. The house on the left was, until the mid 1800s, the Bell Inn. The innkeeper was Mr Lamble who was better known as 'Old Horney'.

The lower half of East Street showing on the right the high wall and barn opposite Summerfield, whilst beyond was the Pound House with its cider press, all now gone. My grandmother, Mrs Kate Farnes, kept Summerfield as a Guest House for many years.

Town Hall Place. In the centre is the house to the left of the shop, now gone, and the garden and entrance to a courtyard behind the shop. The picture was taken around 1900.

Town Cross before its refurbishment as a War Memorial. It was reputedly given by Matilda de Tracey to the town at the time its Borough status was given in 1260, although it is suspected to be of an earlier date.

The cross stood on what was the old Village Green before the Town Hall was built in 1866.

Mary Street as it was in 1905, with the Methodist Chapel on the centre right and the British School on the left. As a lad I recall this street as the one to avoid if possible. The inhabitants used to stand at the doorways and catcall to any unfortunate passers by, often making comments about their appearance.

Upper Fore Street. The house on the extreme left was burnt down in the 1950s. Lower down the street was Frank Hamlin's tiny shop and Bill Brooks' fish shop. Below that was Edwards' fancy goods and newsagents. On the right was Frank Edwards' general store and saddlery and below that was Gale's drapery.

use, Bovey Tracey

The Mission House was built by Canon Courtenay in 1879. It was staffed by the Clewer Sisters and used both as a hospice and for nursing the sick. Bible meetings and Sunday School were also held there and it had a very nice chapel. This building now houses the Job Centre.

Union Square in about 1904. The picture shows the Post Office on the left, an orchard where Lloyds Bank now is, whilst the houses above the Conservative Club were not yet built. On the right is Bond's newsagents shop, later to be Stephen May and Archie Rowe's drapery and haberdashery.

el Square, Bovey Tracey.   Published by T. Cann, Bovey Tracey.

Union Square showing Sercombe's store on the right, with Percy Peters' wine and grocery below and further down, the Temperance Hall.

Union Square in about 1880 showing the Union Hotel on the right with its collonade over the entrance. The proprietor was Mr Wolfinden. The houses on the left have now all gone.

Yew Tree House was originally three houses. With its old porch it dates back to the fifteenth century and was originally thatched, as were most of the houses on the opposite side of the street. In the eighteenth century it was the home of the master of the Grammar School.

Cromwell Arch was formerly the entrance to an ancient monastery of Norman times. The picture shows a mass of ivy on top, with walls to the left and right which were once part of the monastery wall.

Lower Fore Street looking up towards the Union Square, with Upham's hair cutting establishment on the right and Mardons' Beehive grocery store.

The bridge was built in 1642 and was one of the prime objectives of the Roundhead forces in the Civil War battle of 1646. The picture shows the bridge as it was before the footpath was built.

Station Road, Bovey Tracey. (Looking West). Published by T. Cann, Bovey Tracey

Station Road from the bridge. In the distance can be seen the Old Coaching Inn which at that time was a butcher's shop owned by William Bovey. The cottage on the left was occupied by Mr and Mrs Dear and family.

Marsh Cottages. This row of old cottages, between the river and the Marsh Path housed five families, one of which was that of John Short. The cottages were demolished in the First World War.

Bovey Tracey, The Mill.

The building beside the bridge, popularly known as 'The Old Mill' in fact never was a mill! It was built by John Divett in 1854 as stabling and outhouses for his private house, Riverside. The wheel pumped water to the top of the tower, providing gravity-fed water for his house, the first in Bovey to have piped water. The picture above also shows Marsh Cottages on the right.

Bovey Tracey, Coach starting for the Moors.

The Dolphin Hotel in the Dolphin Square was built in the late nineteenth century as a Coaching House and was owned by John Joll. From here horse-drawn wagonettes ran trips over the Moor.

The Railway Hotel, also in the Dolphin Square, was built a little earlier, around 1860, at the same time that the railway came to Bovey Tracey. The proprietor then was Mr J.G. Beer.

Moir & Davie's Garage in the Dolphin Square as it was at the beginning of this century.

Brookside became a tea room about 1945. Prior to this it was owned by Mr Wyatt as a private house.

Heathfield Terrace taken around 1900 with no development on the right hand side. The Toll House can just be seen and the state of the unpaved road is very noticeable.

St John's Church, built by Canon Courtenay in 1851 to enable him to indulge in his High Church leanings, which were frowned upon at the Parish Church. The church was held jointly with the Parish Church during Canon Courtenay's lifetime and was served by him and several Curates.

St John's Cottages were built for the use of the Church of St John in the 1870s.

The Roman Catholic Church. This little galvanised church in Ashburton Road, opposite Moor View houses, was built in 1904 and demolished after 1935 when a new church was built. The interior was quite ornate, in spite of its unprepossessing exterior. Before the original church was built, the nearest Roman Catholic Church was in Chudleigh, and people used to walk there for the 8 a.m. service.

Brimley Road taken at the turn of the century. It comprised just these few houses, the rest was open country.

Five Witches is an old farm on the Haytor Road. The origin of the name is not known, and is now corrupted to Five Wyches.

This was the original Bovey Mill, owned by Mr A.J. Wyatt's mother and then by him from 1870–1910. It stood where the Dartmoor Garage now stands and its wheel was powered by water from the leat which came down from the River Bovey via Parke grounds. After 1910 the new mill was built in its present position. A.J. Wyatt is in the photo holding his daughter's hand.

South Brook Cottages, Bovey Tracey. E 31660

Southbrook and Atway Cottages are very old and are known to have been occupied during the Civil War. Atway Cottages and farm stood astride the old pack-horse trail from Parke to Hennock, parts of which can still be followed and traced.

Attway Cottages, Bovey Tracey. E 3166

BOVEY'S SCHOOLS

We have always been quite well blessed in the matter of education. When the first Grammar School was formed in Fore Street in 1715, there were but a few scholarships for poor children. But with Victorian times, the need for education for the working classes was realised and the churches started their schools, followed by the Council. They provided a good elementary education for everyone, regardless of means.

The Grammar School (1876–1910) was built on a plot given by Mr W.R. Hole, and was both a boarding and a day school. It was a continuation of the old grammar school first founded in Bovey in 1715 and it had a very good scholastic reputation. It closed with the advent of the free schools in Bovey.

The Church School was first formed in 1834 in the room later to be known as the Church Room. It moved to new buildings on the opposite side of the road in 1868 as it became overcrowded. These two photographs show the Girls' School in 1890 and the Boys' School in 1904.

Newscutting from 22 January 1835.

Bovey Tracey. — It is our pleasing duty to announce the opening on Thursday last, in this town, of a new built School house, 40ft. long, by 18ft. wide, to be conducted on the principles of the Church National School society, on a spot of ground given by Francis Berry, Esq., of Barnstaple. The christian philanthropist could not but contemplate with feelings of satisfaction, the completion of such a desirable object, and witness the animated countenances of those who had laboured to consummate this purpose, — and whose looks confirmed their intentions still to labour on in so good a cause. The children were regaled with a plentiful supply of that good old English Fare, roast Beef and Plum-Pudding, given to them by the worthy octogenarian Vicar, who was surrounded by his Parishioners, and by generations that had sprung up during the more than half a century that he has been the incumbent of a parish, where the liberality of his dissenting religious principles has gained him the respect of his dissenting brethren. After an appropriate address by the Rev. P. Smith, the zealous assistant curate, the business of the day was concluded by singing the National Anthem.

The first two photographs show the Girls' School in 1915 with Miss Calloway as Headmistress, and in 1922 as a Mixed School with the teachers Miss Gilbert, Miss Napper, Miss Upham, with the Rev. Barry Hyde in the centre. The third photograph shows the Church School in 1929 when the numbers of pupils had then dropped to only thirty-five.

The pupils in the third picture are as follows; Bill Beer, Alan Mardon, Stan Blackmore, Dick Walker, Bill Peerless, Fred Peerless, Bill Holmes, Violet Evans, Iris Prowse, Joan Irving, Winnie Davey, Margery Lane, Joyce Cann, Eileen Holmes, Margaret Mann, Phyllis Blackmore, Joan Mann, Douglas Cann, Sam Fogwill, Pat Tregoning, Bill Lane, Joyce Jago, Albert Harsent, Peter Pawley, Ernest Harsent and Bill Martin.

The pupils of Brimley School in the 1870s with Miss Treleavan the Headmistress.

In 1900, Mrs Warren was the Headmistress of St John's School, with Mrs Hellyer and Miss Winnie Staddon.

The British School in 1902. It was first opened in 1867 by Miss Annie Croker, to combat the supposed high churchmanship of the Church School. At one time, one of the masters was Mr A.J. Cole (Jan Stewer). This building is now the Gospel Hall.

The British School Annexe was at the bottom of Spion Kop in a wooden hut and was used to accommodate the overflow from the main school. When the Council School opened in 1910, the pupils from the British School formed up in procession and marched down to their new home.

The Council School in 1912. It was first known as the Council School, as distinct from the Church School. The Headmaster was Mr George Lamacraft and the Infant teacher was Miss Martin.

The Council School in 1934. This was the Infants' School and the teacher was Miss Parker. The children in the picture are, from left to right:

Back row, P. Carpenter, L. Moore, V. Coombes, W. Mountford, F. Carpenter, S. Mountford and R. Brimblecombe.

Middle row, W. Ayres, W. Carpenter, H. Payne, C. Carpenter, C. Dixon, R. Ayres, D. Martin, S. Godfrey Wreford, K. Fouracre and L. Steer.

Front row, H. Wills, M. Hooper, B. Beer, D. Brealey, T. Waldron and M. Wills with I. Beer with the ball.

THE BOVEY TRACEY POTTERY

The pottery played a very important part in the working life of the town and from about 1840 onwards was a very large employer. At its height about 250 workers were gainfully employed. It was the largest pottery in the South West making both plain and decorative ware for private sale as well as for the Government.

The pottery was originally known as the Folly Pottery and was an extension of the pottery at Indio. A large proportion of the working population was employed here.

There were sixteen kilns in operation and a mass of buildings (or shops) housing all the various trades. These included pot making, decorating, packing, glazing and many others.

This group of workers was taken around the beginning of the century.

The Higher Mill in 1890. This was the building where the washing and slabbing of the clay was done before being transported to the lower pottery. Several families lived in the upper storey. Jack Webber's family lived there for a while.

These houses in Pottery Road were built especially for the workers, many of whom originally came from Stafford. This photograph was taken in about 1910.

Pottery Pond is a man-made pond, fed from a leat which came all the way from the Becky Brook above Becky Falls. It was used to feed the water wheels at both the higher and lower pottery.

Bluewaters was originally the pit used to obtain clay for the pottery and lignite for the kilns. However, it proved not to be viable. Many seams of clay and lignite were tunnelled underground from this pit. There was a water wheel here which used to pump out the surplus water and to raise the clay. This photograph is dated about 1920.

FESTIVITIES

Festivities of all kinds played a very important part in rural life. In the days of the six-day working week, they provided the working classes with the opportunity to enjoy a little light relief from the everyday burden of work. With no other means of entertainment, home-produced events were a major part of all festivals.

The Town Hall bedecked with bunting, and the crowds gathered for the Coronation of George V in 1911. Standing beside Bobby Finch the policeman on his left, are my grandmother, mother and four of her sisters.

The Coronation Fête at Parke in 1911. Big celebrations were held here to mark the occasion and included teas, races etc.

The Coronation maypole was also part of the celebrations.

The beating of the bounds took place in the same year (1911) also as part of the celebrations.

The Carnival in 1911. This first picture shows Charlie Blackmore and friends with a barrel organ.

Lance Tregoning and Miss Joan Cleave in the 1925 carnival.

A group in the Union Square in the 1920s.

Another group with a lorry. The date is estimated at 1928.

This picture was taken in 1918.

Wyatts lorry decorated in the 1920s.

Bill Blackmore with his horse and milk float in the 1930s. Most of the carnivals until the late 1920s were held in the autumn, but eventually they became summer affairs. The autumn ones were always complete with lighted floats and torchlight processions.

Muriel Clarke, Carnival Queen in the 1930s.

The Black and White Minstrels, organized in the early 1900s by Henry Heath. They were in great demand for concerts all over the area. The artistes used to travel around the villages, firstly by horse charabanc, and later by motors. They were very popular and once broadcast on radio from Plymouth.

G. H. Stone

Pageants were held regularly and were much enjoyed. This photograph was taken at Brimley Cross in the 1930s.

A pageant group in the 1930s at St John's.

This was one of the many pageants organized by Mrs Ursula Ellis, about 1938.

Band of The Rumvoozlers.

Cann & Son, Bovey Tracey.

This photograph of the Bovey Band dates from about 1910. It is entitled 'Rumvooslers' and is taken outside the Cricket Pavilion. It shows the band preparing for the carnival. Some of the faces that can be recognised are Ned Call, Francis King, Charlie Blackmore, Mr Holland and Mr Short.

The Bovey Band was in existence for many years, right up until the 1950s. This picture shows the band in 1938.

Bovey Band in procession on the bridge…   …and in concert in the Town Hall.

Mafeking celebrations in 1900. The brass cannon used for this is clearly shown.

A street party for V.E. Day. This party was organized by the inhabitants of
Priory.

V.E. Day party in the Union Square.

This school band was photographed at the Church School in the early 1900s.

Empire Day in the Church School in the early 1930s.

THE RAILWAY

In its heyday, up until the end of the 1920s, the railway was extensively used by passengers, and also heavily and almost exclusively, for freight and goods.

This photograph shows a general view of the station, taken from Marlborough Terrace about 1910.

These two photographs were taken in 1925 and 1958 respectively. The latter was taken when the passenger service closed. The Station Master in 1958 was Mr Arthur Yendall.

Charabancs waiting at the station to take passengers over the Moors. The picture was taken in 1920.

Passenger train at the station.

The bad floods in 1930 left the station deep under water.

The level crossing over the main road, with Wyatt & Bruce in the background.

WEATHER DISASTERS

The town was always particularly prone to flooding, it was almost an annual event, some years were worse than others. Being so close to the Moors, all excess water found its level, and unfortunately, our town, being low, was in the way. We are fortunate in being just below the recognised snow line, but even so, on occasions life has been completely disrupted.

The lower part of the town has always been subject to flooding. Some of the worst floods occurred in 1890, but unfortunately there is no known pictorial record of this. However, this first picture shows the scene in 1927 with a stalled omnibus being pulled out of the water by another.

This picture was taken in 1930 and shows the rush of water under the bridge with the Marsh Field completely covered.

Harris's Grocery Shop under water in 1930. The occupants are in the upstairs window looking out.

More of the floods in 1930 as a bus tries to get through from the Fore Street end.

The flooding in 1948 was probably the last of the very bad floods. This picture shows one elderly lady having to walk along the wall as even the footpath was flooded.

Parke View Field completely submerged in 1948.

There are unfortunately no pictorial records of the great blizzard of the 1890s. This is Five Wyches Cross under heavy snowfall in 1930.

Both these pictures show the heavy snowfall of 1947 when the town was cut off for several days. The upper picture shows Fore Street, and the other is Orchard Terrace, with John Hydon on the sledge.

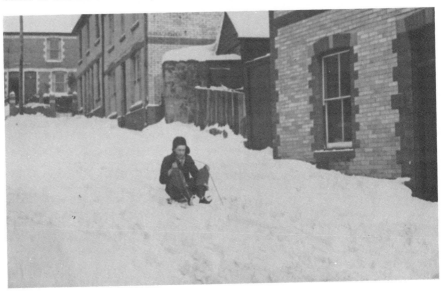

The Baptist Church outing leaving from the Railway Station in 1910. It clearly shows the sort of clothes that were worn to go to the seaside for the annual trip. This outing was a delight – looked forward to by a great many people. For some it was their only outing of the year.

The Parish Church outing in 1948 shows the difference in attire.

WANDERING 1920 BOVANIANS
JUNE 30TH

Most of the Public Houses ran outings as annual events, and for the first part of the century, they were for the men only. It wasn't until the late 1920s that ladies were accepted.

Coaches outside the Union Hotel.

The first of the ladies going on an outing in the late 1920s.

Seaside outing at Teignmouth in the early 1920s.

BOVEY TRACEY'S SHOPS

Until the outbreak of the Second World War the town was almost completely self supporting in its shops and trades. There were five dairies, five bakers and six grocers in the town right up until that time and all trade was confined to the local area. Every type of shop was represented so there was no need to leave the town for goods of any kind.

Sercombe's Saddlery Store in Union Square in about 1900.

Bovey Stores owned by Percy Peters, again in about 1900.

Percy Peters in his car at the rear of the Bovey Stores.

The Co-operative Society in its original position at the beginning of East Street where it joins Town Hall Place. Outside the shop, the Manager Mr George Stephens is in the back row.

Eastmans' Christmas display in 1926. The Manager is Mr W. Wotton. Such a display would probably be frowned upon these days. The boy with the bicycle is Charles Snow.

Tregoning's Grocer's Shop in Town Hall Square in 1922, with Lance Tregoning (the author) in the foreground.

Collins' Cycle Shop in the Union Square in about 1920. Mrs Nancy Collins is in the doorway.

Hamlin's tiny Sweets and Greengrocery shop in Fore Street in 1922.

Mann's Butchers shop was on the other side of the road and is seen here in about 1900. This is the only original shop now left in Bovey. It is a delicatessen.

These two pictures show deliveries from shops. In the first one, Edward Godsland is delivering bread and in the second, Bill Brooks is delivering fish with his horse and trap.

Reg Hodge outside his hairdressing shop in the late 1920s.

THE PARISH CHURCH

The Parish Church is certainly the oldest building in the town. The tower dates back to the thirteenth century, but there was a building on the same spot in Saxon times, probably as early as the seventh century. It was the centre of life right through the centuries, its tower dominates the town and can be seen for miles around, especially at night, when floodlit. The fifteenth-century screen is one of the finest in the South West.

This picture shows the interior of the church before restoration in 1870, with box pews and the pulpit on the opposite side of the screen.

The screen after the removal of the rood and before the restoration of the top of the screen. The South Chapel was not then the Lady Chapel, but held the pews for the Hole family.

The Bellringers in 1911 and 1950. The first photograph shows: *back row* (left to right), Bill Brooks, Mr Olver, Sam Rowe, Charlie Blackmore; *front row* (left to right), Bert Blackmore, Bill Weeks, Mr Nicholls, Mr Bolt and Mr Mitchell.

The second photograph shows: *back row* (left to right), R. Holman, A. Yeo, R. Ballinger, N. Lavis and J. Ellis; *front row* (left to right), Mr Lavercombe, B. Blackmore, W. Brooks, S. Blackmore and J. Heale.

Bert Blackmore and Bill Brooks appear in both pictures.

The Church Choir in 1910 with Rev. Barry Hyde in the centre. The members of the choir are as follows;

1. Frederick Alford
2. Samuel Gale
3. Charles Daymond
4. William Harris
5. George Prescott
6. Edward Nickolls
7. Leonard Mardon
8. William Pring
9. William Prescott
10. George Mardon
11. James Livingstone
12. Melbourne Holman (Choirmaster)
13. Bernard Frost
14. Donald Bowles
15. Harry Payne
16. H.B. Hyde (Vicar)
17. Albert Gale
18. Arthur Weeks
19. Maxwell Daymond
20. Herbert Bowden
21. Leslie Weeks
22. Leslie Bowles
23. Percy Prescott
24. Frank Edward
25. Kenneth Bowles
26. Harold Hamlin

The Choir in 1950 with Rev. G.O.C. Duxbury.

The Mothers' Union in 1919. This picture was taken outside the Church Room.

The panorama as seen from the top of the church tower. It shows the upper part of East Street before the Almshouses were built.

THE FARMING COMMUNITY

Agriculture was one of the mainstays in the economy of the town. Apart from the pottery, agriculture in all its forms was the main employer for the people of Bovey.

An old threshing machine in action.

A ploughing match at Langaller Farm in the early 1930s. Bob Sage is behind the plough, winning the cup for the straightest furrow.

Sheep shearing in the Bovey area in the late 1800s.

The cider press in action on a local farm in 1925.

A break from haymaking. The man holding the cider jug is Bill Blackmore, the bearded man is 'Tiger' Heath.

A hay cart being loaded in 1925.

Haymaking at Atway in the 1950s.

New Park Sawmills at work in the early 1900s.

The forge at Bowdens with a horse being shod in the early part of this century.

Jim Payne at work in his forge in Town Hall Place.

Heath Bros timber yard employees at their annual dinner.

ORGANIZATIONS

The Fire Brigade is by far the oldest organization in Bovey. It began using the hand-drawn Insurance-owned pumps, graduating to the town-owned horse-drawn engine, hand pumped with twelve men a side. Then the various motorised engines followed, all of which, until the 1940s, were purchased by voluntary subscription.

Other organizations which played a large part in the life of the town were the Territorial Army, Civil Defence, Home Guard and R.A.O.B.

The horse-drawn engine at a fire at Luscombe Farm in 1908. The horses had first to be caught and harnessed before the engine could get under way.

The first Dennis motor engine with solid rubber wheels in 1928. It was kept in the building at the rear of the Town Hall, which is now the senior citizens' rest room.

The funeral of a fireman in 1927. The Fire Brigade always turned out to escort the funeral of a comrade. This shows the old oak bier, made by Tucker Bros in the late 1800s. The funeral was of Mr Edward Steer in 1927.

The Queen Mary was the last engine purchased by public subscription. It is shown here being christened by Dame Violet Willis in the 1930s.

The Territorials on parade outside the Town Hall in 1912.

The Royal Antediluvian Order of Buffaloes. In 1935, members used to meet in the back of the Bell Inn. It was very popular, known as 'the working man's Freemasonry'.

Members of the Civil Defence in 1944.

During the War years, the numbers of Special Constables increased considerably.

St John's Ambulance Brigade's first ambulance being blessed at the Cricket Field in 1948. This ambulance was purchased by public subscription.

A view from Mary Street in 1930 across open country, which is now all covered in housing estates.

The view from Ashburton Bridge in 1928. All this land is now covered by Brimley Vale housing estate.

Digging the water mains in Fore Street in 1920. One of the trenches collapsed at one point and Bernard Wills was buried, although he was dug out unharmed. The depth of this hand-dug trench can easily be seen.

Mr William Daymond winding the church clock in the 1940s.

The Parish Church Social Club formed in 1946 and averaged about seventy members. It continued for over twenty-five years and was always very popular.

A ramble by members of Parish Church Social Club in 1947.

The Parish Church Social Club's entry in the carnival in 1948.

Mr Percy Webber on his early 1920s motor bike.

In the early part of this century the family unit was a much recognised part of life, and of course, with travel being restricted, the various generations stayed very much together.

The wedding of the author's parents in 1916.

The Cleave family, carpenters in Fore Street in 1903.

Sam Tolley and his family in their horse and trap.

The Godsland family who had a baker's business in Fore Street.

YOUTH ORGANIZATIONS

Bovey has always had plenty of things for young people to become involved in. As far back as the last century the Parish Church was running a company of the Boys Brigade, which used to meet in the Church Hall. This gave rise to the hall's other name, 'The Brigade Hall'. Unfortunately no photographs seem to exist of this part of the Town's history. Bovey has also had companies of Scouts and Guides over at least the last seventy years.

The first troop of Boy Scouts was formed in 1916 by the Rev. Woods, a curate at the Parish Church, but this closed in a few years. The troop was formed again in 1926 by Mr Reg Hodge. This was a very active company, holding weekly meetings, local summer camps etc. There was also a bugle band as the picture shows. This picture was taken outside Hodge's hairdressing shop in about 1928, with Mr Hodge in the centre.

By the mid 1930s a Rover Troop was formed. This was for the older boys
and George Treen was in charge. This picture was taken on the occasion
of the Silver Jubilee of George V in 1935. A bonfire was built at the top of
Haytor, on the smaller of the two rocks. This was part of a chain of
bonfires around the country.

After an abortive attempt by Miss Wymark Hyde, the daughter of the vicar, to start a company of Girl Guides in 1916, a second company was formed in 1929 by Miss G. Hunter and Miss K. Tolley. This proved very successful. A company of Brownies was also started at the same time under Miss Margaret Sayre and Miss Geraldine Hole.

A district parade by the Guides in East Street. They are on their way to the Parish Church in 1932.

The Guides on a weekend camp in 1932.

A company of Cadets pictured in about 1922. The cadets were re-formed at the outbreak of the Second World War.

RECREATION

There has always been a great interest in sport in the town. Rugby was the original winter sport, but by the 1900s, Association Football had taken over with the advent of the St John's Association Football Club who used to play in a field at the end of Bucks Lane, beside the river. With cricket, Bovey is able to boast the second oldest club in the county, formed in 1852, and also one of the most delightful grounds. The ground was created by the cricketers, from a field that was predominantly gorse and which took many years of hard work to reach its present fine condition. Bowls, tennis and badminton have all played their part in a full selection of sports.

The first ever picture taken of the cricket team in 1895.

Cricket first team in the early 1920s.

The first team later in the 1920s.

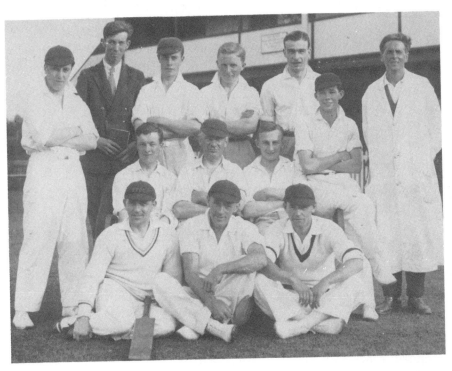

The second team about the same time.

The first team in 1935 with the President, Dr Harrisson in the centre.

A picture of the original pavilion. No photograph exists, but this plate from the Bovey Pottery is on show inside the present pavilion.

The Cricket Club outing to Dartmeet in about 1912.

St John's Association Football Team in about 1910, and in 1935.

Junior Football. The club at the Council School about 1937, with the Headmaster Mr Bint at centre left.

The old-established bowls club. This picture was taken on V.E. Day, 1945.

There was a private tennis club run by the Misses Gurney for St John's, using private courts in the 1930s. Today's club, with their own courts at the Recreation Ground, was formed in 1958. This is the opening.

Cycling was a very popular occupation in the pre-1914 years. A regular club with their own rules, badges, etc. was formed and was very popular in the town.

LOCAL HISTORY TITLES
FROM DEVON BOOKS

Ashburton –
The Dartmoor Town

A detailed account of the history of this ancient stannary town. The author has lived in the Ashburton area for almost forty years and in every chapter he pours out his knowledgeable enthusiasm on every aspect of a thousand years of history. Personalities, buildings, traditions, trade, religion, agriculture, and education are all examined in great depth and in a very readable style. The book is accompanied by numerous photographs and illustrations.

ISBN 0 86114–846–0   £5.95

Old Witheridge

A collection of over two hundred old photographs and newspaper cuttings, covering the last 150 years of the life of the village. Crammed full of stories and anecdotes, *Old Witheridge* is a full and entertaining account of the people and places of days gone by.

ISBN 0 86114–821–5   £6.95

Budleigh Salterton
in Bygone Days

This book is the personal memory of Budleigh Salterton by a long-time resident, Jim Gooding. The story runs from 1904 when he was born in Budleigh, up to the days following the Second World War. Much has changed since those days but Jim's recollections are so vivid that they bring old Budleigh Salterton back to life. Illustrated with over one hundred old photographs.

ISBN 0 86114–811–8   £5.95

All these titles are available through your local bookshop.

For the full list of Devon Books titles send for your free catalogue to: The Publishing Manager, Devon Books, Hennock Road, Marsh Barton, EXETER EX2 8RP. Tel. (0392) 74121.